TRADE

Rob Bowden

Contents

Introduction

Trade is the exchange (buying and selling) of goods or services. It happens every day, all over the world, on both a large and small scale. Examples of trade range from the simple purchase of food from a grocery store to the multi-million dollar purchase of stocks on the global financial markets.

Trade is an activity in which most people participate every day. Each time you buy something from a store, you are trading with the person selling that item. Although most trade today—at both local and global levels—involves the exchange of money, there are other methods of trade as well. Rather than paying for goods or services, they might be directly exchanged for one another. For example, a hairdresser might accept eggs from a farmer in return for cutting the farmer's hair. Before the widespread use of money, all trade was carried out like this.

"Swapping" goods in this way is based on a principle called "comparative advantage." This is where some individuals, communities, or even countries are better placed to provide

▲ A street-side fruit and vegetable market in Marrakech, Morocco. This is an example of basic trading, which performs a vital function in many economies.

▲ Engineers work on a giant electrical generator in a factory in Berlin. Germany has a reputation for high-quality precision engineering, giving it a comparative advantage over other nations in this area.

certain goods or services than others. This may be due to the location of raw materials or because of particular skills. Today, this principle can also be applied to global exchanges of goods or services for money. Certain countries specialize in particular areas. Turkey, for example, is very good at producing textiles; Germany is well known for precision engineering. They have an advantage over other countries, which cannot produce the same goods at the same low prices.

Global Connections

Trade increasingly involves exchanges with distant people and places. Even a simple product such as a tennis ball can involve a complex chain of transactions before it reaches the stores (see page 9). The same is true for a wide range of products, from food, clothing, and stationery to electronics and cars. Services are also becoming more global. It is not uncommon today to call a customer helpline from the United States or Europe and find that the call is answered by someone in India. These connections have come about because of a process known as globalization (see page 8), whereby countries, communities, and individuals are increasingly connected with, and dependent on, one another. This book explores the globalization of trade and its impacts and implications.

Eyewitness

"If trade undermines life, narrows it, or impoverishes it, then it can destroy the world. If trade enhances life, then it can be a better world."
Dame Anita Roddick, founder of the Body Shop

The Globalization of Trade

It is almost impossible to avoid the influence of globalization. It can be seen all around us, from the clothes we wear and the food we eat, to the television we watch and the people we know. Trade plays a pivotal role in this process, but what does globalization really mean?

▲ The cost of traveling has been drastically reduced by low-cost airlines such as easyJet, allowing greater numbers of people to travel further than they could in the past.

A Shrinking World

The basic idea of globalization is that we are living in a smaller, more connected world than ever before. Of course, the world has not really become smaller, but it feels this way because it is more accessible. Developments in technology have made us more aware of events in other countries than ever before. Improvements in communications mean that images of a news story unfolding in one country can be beamed around the world in a matter of minutes—sometimes even seconds. Cell phones and e-mail allow us to communicate with people thousands of miles away. Cheaper cars and the introduction of low-cost flights mean that it is now easier than ever to visit other countries and experience different cultures.

For those living in more economically developed countries (MEDCs), it can be easy to take all this for granted. It is important to

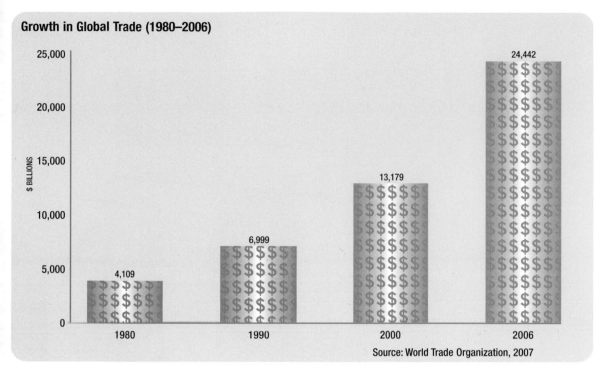

Growth in Global Trade (1980–2006)

$BILLIONS

- 1980: 4,109
- 1990: 6,999
- 2000: 13,179
- 2006: 24,442

Source: World Trade Organization, 2007

▲ Global trade has grown at a dramatic rate in recent years, and is now worth nearly six times as much as it was in 1980.

remember, however, that the technological revolution has not taken place at the same rate all over the world. As a result, some countries have benefited more than others from globalization.

Trade Goes Global

Globalization has had a huge impact on trade—in both good and bad ways. For example, globalization means that companies can now base themselves almost anywhere in the world, allowing them to reach new markets. This can be good news for the company, but it may have disadvantages for communities in the host country. Technologies like the Internet have also resulted in new types of trade. A good example of this is eBay, which allows people to buy and sell from one another. Started in the U.S. in 1995, eBay now operates in 33 countries with 181 million registered users. In 2005, it traded more than $44.3 billion worth of goods—around $1,511 every second!

Focus on...
A Global Journey

The journey of a typical tennis ball from creation to consumer demonstrates how complex the globalization of trade has become. The balls are made at a factory in the Philippines, but their story involves a trade spanning four continents. Sulphur from Korea, silica from Greece, magnesium carbonate from Japan, zinc oxide from Thailand, and clay from the U.S. are all used to help give the rubber (from Malaysia and the Philippines) its bounce. The cloth is made from New Zealand wool, shipped 11,800 miles (19,000 km) to the UK, where it is woven before traveling 6,700 miles (10,800 km) back to Asia. Once made, the balls are packaged in cans from Indonesia, before finally being shipped for sale around the world.

▲ The world-famous tea clipper the *Cutty Sark* would once have been the very latest in technology. Such vessels allowed for a dramatic increase in the speed of trade in comparison with transporting goods by land.

Trade in Ancient Times

Although globalization has taken place at a dramatic rate over the past 50 years, trade at a global level is in fact nothing new. As long ago as 3000 B.C., civilizations such as the Mesopotamians and ancient Egyptians were trading with countries far away from their own. People would travel great distances overland, carrying goods such as spices that were valuable trading commodities (any item that can be bought or sold). One of the best-known trade routes of ancient times was the Silk Road. It connected China through India, Pakistan, and central Asia to Europe and North Africa. The Silk Road was at its peak from around 200 B.C., but by around A.D. 1600 ships had become a much faster and more efficient way of transporting goods for trade, and overland routes like the Silk Road became less important. This is an early example of how developments in technology have changed the way trade is carried out and have played a big part in globalization.

Trade and Society

The impact of trade on different societies is often only thought of in terms of the money it generates. In fact, the process of trade has had much wider implications. As people began to venture further afield to trade their goods and services, they took with them beliefs and traditions from their own cultures and learned about those of other societies.

Over the years, these influences sometimes became absorbed into the cultures of people far away. For example, trade was one of the ways in which the Arabic language and the Islamic religion spread to North Africa. Islam also spread through trade to become the dominant religion of Indonesia. Today there are more Muslims (followers of Islam) there than in any other country.

Have Your Say

Trade can often be followed by migration, as people move around to take up jobs created by the spread of trade to different countries.

- As trade becomes more global, is it likely that we will see similar patterns in migration?
- What are the positive and negative impacts of trade-related migration?
- Is the link between migration and trade purely historical or is it still important today?

The social impacts of globalization in trade can still be seen today. Migration—the movement of people from one country to another—is a good example of this. As trade becomes more global, people move around the world to take advantage of the employment opportunities it creates. As they do so, they take elements of their culture with them.

Migrants do not simply follow trade, however; they can also create it. This can take the form of generating a market for a particular type of food, for example, or the form of money that is sent home to support family members (remittances). In total, global remittance payments in 2005 were estimated to be around $230 billion.

Lessons from the Past

The social impact of trade in the past can also help explain the problems experienced by some countries today. In the past, several European nations owned colonies in Africa. They would obtain the raw resources available in those colonies (such as cotton or cocoa) cheaply and would then create products from them that could be traded around the world at much higher prices.

Top 10 Remittance Recipients (2006)

Country	Payments (in $ billion)
India	26.9
Mexico	24.7
China	22.5
Philippines	14.9
France	12.6
Spain	8.9
United Kingdom	7.3
Belgium	7.2
Germany	6.7
Bangladesh	5.5

Source: World Bank

The Difficulties of Adding Value

The process of taking a basic material and turning it into something that can be exported at a higher price is called "adding value." It is one of the areas in which there is great inequality between countries today. Parts of Africa are rich in resources such as gold and diamonds, but they do not have the infrastructure to be able to add value themselves (for example by making a diamond ring that can then be sold for much more than the original materials were worth). In many cases, MEDCs create the product and therefore benefit from the added value.

This situation has worsened recently because the price of many important resources has dropped. For example, cotton halved in value between the mid-1990s and 2003. By 2005, it had fallen a further 30 percent, plunging millions of African cotton farmers into poverty.

Eyewitness

"How can we cope with this problem? Cotton prices are too low to keep our children in school, or to buy food and pay for health. Some farmers are already leaving. Another season like this will destroy our community."

Brahima Outtara, cotton farmer in Burkina Faso

Subsidizing Trade

One of the reasons that cotton prices have dropped is the increased level of subsidies—money given to support a particular industry—paid by the U.S. government to its cotton farmers. Subsidies have encouraged them to produce more cotton, which in turn means that there is a lot available on the world market. This causes the price of cotton to drop. The result is that cotton farmers in less economically developed countries (LEDCs),

▼ A farmer harvests cotton in northern Nigeria, but, like many West African cotton farmers, the price he is paid for his cotton is out of his control.

▲ Tokyo is one of the most affluent places in the world, a temple to consumption, fashion, and entertainment.

Focus on...
Measuring Trade

Measuring trade is a difficult process. It is very complicated, for example, to record the value of trade that is conducted illegally (such as trade in drugs or weapons). Trade within companies may also not be recorded. Even where information about trade transactions is available, it can be very complex. One of the most useful measures introduced to help with this is "merchandise trade." This is the value of all goods entering (imports) or leaving (exports) a country. In 1950, total merchandise exports were $62 billion, and total merchandise imports were $64 billion. By 1990, these had increased to $3,475 billion, and $3,550 billion, respectively. Trade grew rapidly in the 1990s, and by 2005, exports were $10,434 billion, and imports stood at $10,685 billion.

such as Burkina Faso—where two million people depend on cotton for their livelihoods—are unable to compete.

Critics of globalization argue that examples like this highlight the unfairness of the world trade system and show how more developed regions (such as North America, Europe, Japan, or Australia) misuse their wealth and political power to distort trade. Others argue that countries should be free to protect their own trade and to compete on the global market. There are ongoing debates about how free or fair global trade really is.

World Merchandise Imports and Exports (1960–2005)

	Merchandise exports (current $)	Merchandise imports (current $)
1960	126,583,338,723	133,027,335,874
1965	184,246,937,719	192,730,888,993
1970	309,050,311,748	320,967,700,923
1975	859,854,811,876	884,384,038,224
1980	1,997,673,726,528	2,033,358,129,494
1985	1,906,750,540,399	1,964,900,775,382
1990	3,474,777,775,306	3,549,584,572,124
1995	5,169,878,405,740	5,222,471,545,385
2000	6,452,221,606,172	6,649,619,627,775
2005	10,433,971,209,377	10,684,930,355,288

Source: World Bank

Locally Global and Globally Local

World trade is measured in billions of dollars, and this can make it difficult to see the connection between global trade and daily life. However, even before you leave home in the morning you have been in contact with people you have never met, who live in places you have never been. These connections might not always be obvious, but they can be very important.

Consumer Power

A North American or a European enjoying a cup of tea or coffee for breakfast might find that their drink connects them to people working for low pay and long hours on a tea estate in Sri Lanka or a coffee plantation in Brazil. However, it could just as easily connect them to community-managed tea and coffee operations, where farmers are paid a fair price for their produce—a price that means they can easily meet the needs (education, health care, shelter, food) of their families. In this way, personal choices can make a big difference to people, cultures, and environments around the world. Even the largest global corporations ultimately depend

▼ Even if you shop in a large supermarket, the choices you make can guide the type of produce that big businesses put on their shelves.

Eyewitness

"Twenty million farmers in 50 countries on or around the Equator rely solely on coffee for their livelihoods. Imagine what a difference could be made to those 20 million people if we all drank Fairtrade coffee, especially in countries like Ethiopia, where coffee accounts for over half of foreign-exchange earnings."

Rebecca Seal, "Can consumer power save lives?" *Observer Food Monthly*

on the choices of individual consumers for the success or failure of their businesses. Consumers, therefore, have great potential to influence the behavior and actions of companies through the trade choices they make. This is known as consumer power.

A Confusing Picture

Some consumers choose what to buy with very little thought for the effects of their decision. They make choices based on color, style, taste, and price. They may not even be aware of the environmental impacts of their choice, or whether the people who made that product are treated fairly. Even when consumers want to think about these issues, it can often be difficult to find the information. Labeling programs such as the Fairtrade certificate—used on products that guarantee producers a fair price—can help (see page 38), but for many consumers, it remains a confusing picture.

This confusion can be made worse by the incredible range of products now available. The globalization of trade—made possible by reductions in the cost of transportation and trading over the Internet—means that even very small businesses can have a global presence. In many supermarkets, it is now possible to find coffee produced by small, local village cooperatives, alongside coffee from major brands such as Folgers. The same is true for a growing range of products and services.

▼ Shoppers at a market in Berlin. By understanding more about how and where food is produced, we have the power to influence trade on a global level.

▲ The do-it-yourself store B&Q is one of several retail giants to have begun opening stores in China as part of its global expansion program.

They say that globalization has allowed large companies to dominate the market and drive out local producers and suppliers, resulting in less choice. In Europe, large music stores such as HMV or Virgin, for example, have been blamed for the closure of many independent music retailers. The larger companies were able to offer music at lower prices and could afford expensive advertising campaigns and promotions. As globalization continues, however, these music giants are becoming increasingly challenged themselves by the growing popularity and lower cost of downloading music from the Internet.

The domination of large companies can be seen in many different markets, including books, groceries, hardware, furniture, and electrical goods. Wal-Mart, the U.S. retail giant, is a good example of this. Wal-mart uses its power to continually branch out into new markets such as music or fashion. The result is that many shopping districts are beginning to look the same at both national and, increasingly, international levels.

The Rise of the Retail Giant

Although it may seem as though there are many more products to choose from than there were in the past, there are some people who argue that this is not actually the case.

Choice and Change

There are some areas of trade, however, in which there is clearly more choice. Food in particular is an area in which globalization has resulted in a wide variety of options for

▲ Those against globalization argue that it has resulted in main streets and shopping malls looking the same, whether they are in London, New York, or Tokyo.

Have Your Say

There may be talk of choice, but the reality of average shopping malls is that they all look the same. Where are the local specialty retailers?

- Do you think you have more choice as a consumer or simply more choice of where to purchase the same thing?
- Why might a reduction in choice be bad for trade and the economy?
- What do you think local stores could do to try to survive against major global companies?

consumers, and they are now becoming more selective and better informed. Small companies can use this interest to provide products that set them apart from the competition. This might be in terms of quality or perhaps ethical or environmental standards. These initiatives can challenge the comparative advantage (see page 6) of larger companies and force changes in the marketplace as a whole.

The growth in demand for Fairtrade tea and coffee, for example, has led many mainstream companies to introduce their own Fairtrade produce. Similarly, many supermarkets have introduced their own organic ranges of food to compete with smaller specialty suppliers. These examples show how the globalization of trade, combined with the power of the consumer, can encourage positive changes.

▼ This table shows the 10 largest global retail companies and their sales.

Top 10 Global Retailers

Company	Sales in $ billion (2006)
1. Wal-Mart Stores (United States)	348.65
2. Home Depot (United States)	90.84
3. Costco Wholesale Corporation (United States)	62.42
4. Target Corporation (United States)	59.49
5. Sears Holdings (United States)	53.01
6. Walgreens (United States)	49.22
7. Lowe's Cos (United States)	46.93
8. CVS (United States)	43.81
9. Aeon (Japan)	38.23
10. Best Buy (United States)	33.73

Source: Forbes Lists, 2007

The Bigger Picture

Trade offers many opportunities for communities around the world to greatly improve their lives, but even good trading practices can have unforeseen consequences. In Kenya's Rift Valley, for example, flowers and organic vegetables are grown so that they can be exported to countries in Europe and the Middle East. This trade has become one of Kenya's most important sources of income. In many cases, the workers are treated well, and their families are provided with valuable services, such as health care and education. However, the farms on which the flowers and vegetables are grown are owned by a few wealthy individuals—sometimes people who are not Kenyan. This means that the benefits to the wider community can be limited.

These farms use some of Kenya's most fertile land to grow products that will be exported, while communities elsewhere in the country depend on imported food aid for their survival. Most controversially, the farms use vast quantities of water from nearby Lake Naivasha. There are concerns not only about the impact this is having on the local environment, but also on the amount of water available for local use. Other factors to consider are the emissions and "food miles" (the distance traveled) involved in transporting the goods from the farms to the supermarkets where they will be sold. This shows just how complicated issues of global trade can be and demonstrates how decisions made by consumers on a daily basis can affect people in distant locations.

Global Trade in Services

When trading goods, there is at least some opportunity to trace and measure its impact. Trade in services can be more difficult to monitor and control, as the services may be provided by many different companies or by a group of companies acting together.

Trade in services such as banking, insurance, travel, and technical support have become increasingly globalized. It is now relatively simple to book a vacation apartment directly

▼ Kenyan flower farms were once known for their poor working conditions, but recently several of them have become part of the fair-trade movement, and local communities and individuals have benefited greatly.

▲ Water is a basic human need and has become the subject of great controversy in recent years, as global companies seek to gain control of water supplies in poor economies, such as here in Uganda.

with the owners, rather than having to book through a travel agent, for example. Low-cost telecommunications have allowed banking, insurance, and public-utility (such as gas or electricity) companies to establish telephone support centers anywhere in the world, taking advantage of lower wages in LEDCs.

In many parts of the world, private companies are now competing to run essential services such as water supplies, waste collection, and even education and health care. This is a controversial issue. Many people believe that such services are basic human rights and should not be left in the hands of private companies, which can then place whatever price they like on these services. When private companies tried to take control of the water supply in Bolivia's cities, thousands found themselves without water because they simply could not afford it. Protests forced the Bolivian government to reverse the contracts given to the foreign water companies.

Eyewitness

"The global scandal of water privatization needs to be brought into the open. Multinationals have scoured the world looking for opportunities to profit, while poor communities have repeatedly lost out on access to clean water. The people of Bolivia have delivered a resounding 'no' to water privatization, and this must be respected."
John Hilary, director of campaigns and policy at the charity War on Want

"The real issue is what gets greater access to water to people all over the world, and after decades of trying to improve water systems, we come to the realization that somebody has to pay for the water; it's either consumers through user fees, or it's governments through subsidies. But governments all over the world have either found it impossible to raise consumer tariffs or impossible to provide subsidies. Neither the public sector nor the private sector can invest when nobody pays."
Michael Klein, vice-president for private-sector development, World Bank

The World Trade System

The term "free trade" is often used to describe the system of global trade in use today, and was first made popular in a book called *The Wealth of Nations*, published by Adam Smith in 1776. Smith believed that all the trading laws at the time were preventing countries from improving their economies. He argued that if individuals and economies were free to better themselves (through trade), then the whole of society would benefit. This idea is directly linked with ideas of comparative advantage (see page 6), and free trade has become the basis of modern economic thought.

How Free Is Global Trade?

The realities of global trade are often quite different from the principles of free trade. In 2004, for example, the U.S. textile industry convinced the government to place a quota (limit) on the number of socks being imported from China. They were worried that the influx of cheaper Chinese socks would stop U.S. companies from making money. Similar quotas are found in virtually all forms of trade. This is because trade is directly related to employment and economic growth, which governments are keen to protect in their own countries.

However, there are those who argue that quotas can have a negative effect on the economies they are designed to protect. Limiting the number of imported socks from China to protect local manufacturers removes the element of competition that can keep standards high. The local suppliers may feel that they do not need to improve their product or efficiency. In the long term, this lack of competition may result in job losses and even factory closures.

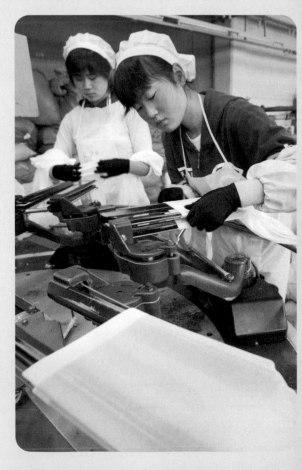

▲ Workers at a sock factory in China; the socks are exported to countries such as the U.S. and those of the European Union.

Subsidies such as those paid to U.S. cotton farmers (see page 12) are another way in which trade can be distorted. Subsidies are payments made by governments to producers or businesses in order to support their activities. The United States, the European Union (EU), and Japan have all been criticized for the amount of subsidies they provide for the agricultural industry. In Europe, dairy farmers receive subsidies equivalent to $2.50 per cow per day. This is more than the $2 per day that around half the world's six billion people struggle to live on. Subsidies can allow countries to produce certain goods that they would not normally be able to, and to flood the global market with these products. This lowers world prices and can cause severe hardship for producers in countries that are not protected by government subsidies.

Eyewitness

"We expect our government to do its job and defend what is left of our domestic sock industry from predatory trade practices, such as we are experiencing with Chinese sock imports."
Charles Cole, chairman, Hosiery Association Domestic Manufacturers Committee, June 29, 2004

"Today's decision [to introduce the sock quota] only perpetuates the failed protectionist policies that have discouraged the U.S. textile industry from becoming competitive, innovative and responsive to their customers, which in turn has exacerbated job losses in the industry."
Laura E. Jones, executive director, U.S. Association of Importers of Textiles and Apparel, October 23, 2004

▼ In countries of the European Union, dairy farmers are granted subsidies based on how many cows they have. The subsidies put farmers in countries that do not have them at a disadvantage.

▲ Every day, companies on trading floors all over the world buy goods, stocks, and shares. Transactions worth billions of dollars can take place at the touch of a button.

The Pace of Trade

Computers and telecommunications have dramatically increased the pace of global trade. The same technological developments have allowed for enormous increases in the volume of trade. In April 2006, for example, the average trade in foreign currency was $2.7 trillion per day—a 37 percent increase from the previous April, and more than double the amount of trade in 2001.

Increases in the speed and volume of trade are generally beneficial, as they improve the efficiency of the global economy. Occasionally, however, they can combine to have negative effects. In 1997, concerns about the growth and stability of Thailand's economy led some investors to begin withdrawing their money from the Thai economy. Other investors felt less comfortable about their own investments and began to do

the same; investments were taken away from other economies in the region. The speed and ease with which this process took place forced banks and businesses to close almost overnight and resulted in a huge financial crisis. In Southeast Asia, thousands of people lost their jobs, and a recession began. Because globalization has resulted in closer links between all trading countries, the effects of the crisis were felt all over the world.

Trade Rules

Many people believe that the Asian financial crisis could have been avoided if there had been tighter rules governing trade in foreign exchange. In fact, the debate about trade rules is not new, and individual governments have been imposing rules on trade to protect their own countries for centuries. As globalization continues, however, it has become more important to establish a set of trade rules that are fair to everyone, all over the world. The first attempt at creating such a set of rules was the General Agreement on Tariffs and Trade (GATT), which was established in 1948. This organization was set up to reduce the barriers and tariffs to trade and make it easier for countries to trade with one another around the world. As the volume and variety of goods and services traded at a global level increased, GATT had to adapt to meet the new needs. The last round of GATT meetings, known as the "Uruguay round," lasted from 1986 to 1994. The negotiations were so complicated that it was decided a new international trade body should be created to oversee the future of global trade. This new body is now known as the World Trade Organization.

Focus on...
The World Trade Organization

The World Trade Organization (WTO) came into being on January 1, 1995. The main purpose of the WTO is to set a series of rules for international trade. As of January 2007, 150 countries were members of the WTO. All these countries have agreed to the rules set by the organization and can bring disputes or appeals against the rules to the WTO. As well as enforcing existing rules, the WTO is involved in negotiating new agreements. Unlike GATT, which was mainly involved in trade in goods, the WTO also oversees trade in services and in knowledge and inventions (intellectual property).

▼ Representatives of the World Trade Organization meet in Hong Kong in 2005 to continue discussions about global free trade.

Does the WTO Work?

Countries join the WTO because they believe it will help improve their trading position. China became a WTO member in 2001 and has benefited enormously because other members can now be forced to let Chinese goods into their countries. Under the rules of the WTO, any country refusing to do so can be punished by trade sanctions. In 2003, for example, the European Union complained about the taxes that the U.S. government had placed on steel. The EU claimed that these taxes were illegal under the rules of the WTO. After an investigation, the U.S. removed the import taxes so they would not have to face sanctions.

Critics of the WTO argue that the existing rules might work for large and powerful trading partners such as the United States, countries of the European Union, Japan, or

Eyewitness

"In theory, the WTO is democratic, and each member has one vote. But in practice, the WTO is quite undemocratic, and poor countries are subject to bullying and exclusion from key discussions and decision making. Over 30 developing countries have no negotiators at the WTO headquarters. Other poor countries have only one negotiator, who has the impossible task of attending over 1,000 WTO meetings a year."
Make Poverty History website

China, but they do little for smaller economies. The fear of sanctions from smaller economies would not seriously threaten a large economy like the U.S. or Japan, and so rich countries may simply ignore such rulings. The way in which rulings are made is also criticized as being secretive, as it takes place behind closed doors. The concern is that wealthy nations,

▼ These people in Indonesia are protesting against the World Trade Organization during WTO meetings in Jakarta in 2007.

which account for the bulk of world trade, may have too much influence in such meetings.

Agricultural subsidies are often used to illustrate these concerns. In the U.S. in 2007, the production costs of cotton were around $0.75 per pound ($1.65 per kg), compared to $0.22 per pound ($0.48 per kg) in Burkina Faso. However, U.S. subsidies meant that farmers could sell their cotton for less. Many LEDCs complained about this system, and the WTO has supported some of these complaints. In 2005, it said that U.S. cotton subsidies were illegal.

Rules vs. Principles

In February 2006, the WTO ruled that the EU must allow genetically modified (GM) food produced in the U.S. to be sold in Europe. Several EU countries have expressed

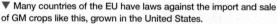

Have Your Say

Many people argue that agricultural subsidies are unfair and should be abolished.

- How might farmers in wealthy nations be affected by the removal of subsidies?
- Why might agriculture be treated differently from trade in other goods and services?
- Are there some agricultural products that should not be subject to trade rules?

serious concerns about GM produce and have their own laws banning them. They are concerned about the potential health and environmental risks that might come with genetic modification. The WTO ruling appears to ignore these concerns, and some countries will be forced to change their laws. Consumer groups and several EU countries have said they will resist the ruling and continue with their opposition to GM produce.

▼ Many countries of the EU have laws against the import and sale of GM crops like this, grown in the United States.

▲ Sales from Wal-Mart's global chain of stores mean that its income is greater than that of many countries.

Company or Country?

Globalization has allowed companies based in one country to grow and move into other countries. These are known as transnational corporations (TNCs), and many of them are now wealthier than major economies. Some have become very powerful influences on global trade. With annual sales in 2006–07 of around $348.65 billion, for example, the U.S.-based Wal-Mart would be the 20th richest economy in the world if it was a country—ahead of countries such as Turkey, Saudi Arabia, Israel, Norway, and South Africa.

TNCs have often been criticized for having too much influence over governments. Globalization has made these companies very wealthy, so governments are often eager for them to invest in their economies. Investment by a TNC could bring employment and economic development to a region. As a result, governments might be prepared to change existing trade rules or ignore certain activities or practices to encourage such investment. In reality, the criticism of TNCs often focuses on a few high-profile examples. Many TNCs have brought wealth and employment to local economies and have been welcomed by governments and communities alike.

Missing Out

One of the main criticisms of TNCs is that profits from their activities and trade often leave the country they are operating in and so do not benefit local communities. Many countries have established special zones where TNCs are allowed to operate at low or even zero tax rates. These zones are attractive to foreign investors, but because they do not have to pay taxes, the benefits for the host country are limited. It may even end up costing the host countries, as they have to provide basic services such as access roads and waste collection. Supporters of these zones point out that any negative impacts are balanced by the creation of jobs and the

Focus on...
Trading Blocs

The World Trade Organization is the main international body governing world trade, but there are several regional organizations known as trading blocs that have their own trade agreements. These trade blocs include the European Union (EU), the North American Free Trade Agreement (NAFTA), the Association of South East Asian Nations (ASEAN), and the Economic Community of West African States (ECOWAS). The purpose of these and other trading blocs is to improve trade by removing barriers such as tariffs or quotas. This is beneficial to countries within the region, but can present more obstacles to trade for countries outside it.

development of skills for local workers. TNC activities can also create demand for local goods and services such as food, shelter, and entertainment for those working for them.

TNCs can relocate their production centers relatively quickly. They might move to take advantage of cheaper labor or because of changes in local laws or tax systems that make their business less profitable. Even a change in the rate of foreign exchange can be enough for some forms of production to shift. Not all production can shift quickly, though. A car plant, for example, is a major investment, but a call center can be set up rapidly because of the low cost of telephones and computers.

▼ Western companies can locate call centers in developing countries such as India relatively quickly and cheaply. This creates jobs for local people, but often the profits do not stay in the host country.

Winners and Losers

The very word globalization implies a process that is taking place across the whole world, and to some extent that is true. Every country is affected by globalization in some way, but when it comes to trade, the process is extremely uneven. Patterns of foreign-exchange transactions (the buying and selling of foreign currency) are a good illustration of this. In April 2006, 32.4 percent of all foreign-exchange transactions took place in the UK, 18.2 percent in the U.S. and 7.6 percent in Japan. Just three countries accounted for almost two-thirds of the global foreign-exchange market.

▲ A meeting of the OECD nations in France. This organization includes 22 high-income nations.

OECD and HIPC

Similar patterns can be seen in merchandise trade (the import and export of goods). In 2005, 60 percent of global merchandise exports came from the 22 high-income nations of the OECD (Organization for Economic Cooperation and Development). The OECD includes the countries of North America and Western Europe, together with Japan, South Korea, Australia and New Zealand. Germany and the U.S. alone accounted for around 9 percent of global exports each. Imports showed a similar pattern, with 65 percent going to OECD nations.

There is a stark contrast between the OECD countries and the 38 countries that make up the HIPC (Heavily Indebted Poor Countries). Between them, the HIPC nations accounted for just 0.5 percent of merchandise exports and 0.65 percent of imports in 2005.

Globalization—Not for Everyone

Supporters of globalization say that this huge difference shows that trade creates wealth, and argue that this can only be a good thing. Critics of globalization say that because these huge differences already exist, LEDCs will find it almost impossible to compete on a global scale—they are simply too small. In fact, the situation is not so straightforward, as the choices of major international investors can dramatically change the trading and economic prospects of a country.

Have Your Say

It could be argued that inequalities in trade are inevitable in a global system built on principles of free trade.

- How much do you think inequalities are a natural part of the system?
- Does history have something to teach us about the global distribution of trade?
- Do organizations like the WTO and trading blocs like the EU reinforce or break down inequalities in global trade?

China is a good example of a poor country that has been helped by investment. In 1990, its merchandise exports were around 1.7 percent of the global total. During the 1990s, there was huge international investment into China and its share of global exports increased to 7.3 percent by 2005—greater than that of Japan, France, or the UK. Over the same period, average incomes in China increased from $320 to $1,740 per year, and the economy grew at an average of just under 10 percent a year. The OECD nations grew by less than 2.4 percent a year.

▼ China's economy is now booming, as can be seen in the huge development of Shanghai, which is fast becoming a city of global importance.

▲ The chairmen of Exxon and Mobil announce their plans for a merger in December 1998.

Corporate Winners

Through the globalization of trade, TNCs have become enormously wealthy and influential, and they are one of the driving forces behind the continued growth of globalization. In the past, TNCs grew by setting up in different parts of the world, reaching new markets. This is how products like Coca Cola and Pepsi became global brands—as likely to be found for sale in remote Himalayan villages as in American convenience stores. This type of physical expansion can be expensive, however, and can be risky for some companies, products, and areas.

An alternative way for companies to expand is to buy or merge with an existing company that is already established in a different market. Many of today's major TNCs have developed and grown as a result of mergers and acquisitions (buying another company). The petrochemical company ExxonMobil, for example, was formed as the result of a merger in 1998 between the two companies Exxon and Mobil. After merging, they could each reduce their costs by combining their operations. Similar "cost-cutting" mergers have happened in the automotive industry, as companies that once competed against each other have joined forces in the hope of increasing their share of the market. This sort of merger and acquisition is often referred to as "horizontal integration" because it involves similar companies joining together.

In 2004, NBC and Vivendi Universal Entertainment merged to form one of the world's largest media and entertainment companies—NBC Universal. This merger was partly an effort to cut costs, but more significantly, it brought different interests and

▲ Universal theme park in Osaka, Japan, is an example of how companies have diversified into many different activities as a result of globalization.

market sectors together. The new company can now produce a film in its own studios, with its own production company, and then advertise it on its own television channels, and show it through its own chain of movie theaters. This style of merger and acquisition is often known as "vertical integration" because it is about different sectors of a business joining forces so they can expand into each other's markets.

When Is Big too Big?

Deals like mergers and acquisitions have to be investigated thoroughly before they are allowed to go ahead. It is important to find out if the new larger company will have too much power and influence in the marketplace. In 2004, cellular company AT&T Wireless tried to buy Cingular Wireless, another cellular phone company. This merger would make AT&T the largest cellular provider in the U.S. The merger was approved, but only after some conditions were agreed to. The combined companies were told to sell some cellular customer contracts and airwave licenses in markets where the deal would mean there was no "real" competition.

Eyewitness

"Companies were no longer interested in merely being the biggest studio or the most successful TV network. They had to be more. Theme parks, cable networks, radio, consumer products, books, and music all became prospects for their potential empires. Media land was gripped by merger mania. If you weren't everywhere… you were nowhere."

Michael J. Wolf, author of *The Entertainment Economy*

No Competition

One of the biggest criticisms of globalization and trade is that it can have negative effects on local businesses. Large TNCs are able to use their great wealth to drive local competitors out of business. One of the clearest examples of this is the growth in branded coffee outlets, particularly the well-known Starbucks chain. Starbucks has a policy of clustering its coffee shops in locations that are popular with its target customers. This is why in some major cities it can seem as though there is a Starbucks on almost every corner. Each coffee shop may not make a great deal of money, but together they dominate the market and drive out independent businesses. Starbucks increased its shops from 275 (then only in parts of the U.S.) in 1993 to 1,900 in 12 countries by 1999. By May 2007, Starbucks had 13,728 outlets in 40 countries.

Focus on...
Offshoring

The opportunities presented by the Internet and cheap phone calls are now supporting a new wave of relocations in services such as customer support and telemarketing. This is known as offshoring. It is estimated that by 2006, the U.S. had lost more than 500,000 service-sector jobs to offshoring. This is expected to increase to around 3.3 million by 2015. A similar number of jobs have been lost in Western Europe, and the trend is continuing. One of the countries that has benefited from offshoring is India. There is a large number of well-educated, English-speaking graduates who are willing to work for up to 70 percent less than people in the U.S. or the UK. China, South Africa, the Philippines, Poland, and Russia are some of the other countries with fast-growing offshore industries.

▼ Many companies now place work abroad. The U.S. company Nike outsources contracts to independent companies overseas. This factory in China produces Nike trainers.

▲ Starbucks has expanded rapidly since the mid-1990s to become a truly globally recognized brand. This outlet is in Beijing near the Forbidden City, which many tourists visit.

Skills and Employment

The growth in trade of a TNC like Starbucks can create local employment opportunities, as the jobs offered are relatively low-skilled. The same is true for many jobs in retail and manufacturing. However, other sectors such as information technology, biotechnology, and engineering require specific skills. The cost (and time) involved in training people to perform those jobs is often very high. This means that rather than invest in local communities, a company may simply bring in skilled labor from outside. This can benefit local businesses by creating a demand for food, clothing, and accommodation, but the influx of higher earning workers can also have negative effects. In many places, it has led to a sudden rise in property prices, making accommodation too expensive for local people. It also means there is little long-term investment in the local community, as many foreign workers will send their earnings home.

Relocations

Globalization has made it relatively easy for companies to relocate their operations to match trading conditions. Lower labor costs, the benefits of working in special zones (see page 26), or a merger with another company can all mean companies want to relocate. This can be good news for communities in the new location, but what about those left behind? If a major company chooses to relocate a factory or service center, hundreds of people could lose their jobs. This might reduce the amount of money in the economy and could lead to other businesses having to close. Since the 1970s, many wealthier nations have suffered periods of high unemployment as large companies have relocated to take advantage of cheaper production centers abroad.

Eyewitness

"Globalization has made a real difference to the quality of life of working people in the UK and across the world, but there are victims as well as winners. Too many British workers are losing their jobs when companies move abroad or fail to compete. Cheap DVD players and clothes are scant compensation if you are being downgraded to poor-quality, insecure, low-paid work."
Brendan Barber, general secretary, TUC (Trades Union Congress)

▲ Hyundai cars waiting to be exported at a shipyard in South Korea. South Korea is an example of a country where investment in education has led to a booming economy in a very short time.

Creating Winners

One of the reasons that India has been so successful in attracting foreign service businesses is its good education system. By investing in education, India has been able to produce a workforce that is as qualified as that in Europe, North America, or Japan, but at a much lower cost. Other nations that have made education a priority have also benefited from the globalization of trade. An educated workforce means that companies do not have to pay for training locals, or for bringing in their own staff. It also means that local people are more likely to be offered jobs and

gain skills that can later be used to develop local businesses. In places such as South Korea, Taiwan, Singapore, and Hong Kong, this model of development has helped to create some major world companies, including Hyundai and Samsung.

Reforming the Systems

Well-educated workforces and special economic zones may help to unlock global trade for some countries, but it remains just that—a select few. In sub-Saharan Africa, many countries struggle to provide even a basic education, let alone one of international standards. For these countries, global trade may only be opened up if the basic systems existing there are reformed and restructured. This would mean organizations like the WTO offering better opportunities for LEDCs. The latest round of WTO talks, which began in 2001, is intended to find ways of helping trade benefit LEDCs, in particular through opening up trade in agriculture. A study by the OECD suggested that if world agricultural tariffs and subsidies were reduced by 50 percent, it would force a major reorganization of global trade in agriculture.

In theory, this could be good news for LEDCs. It would help them regain the comparative advantage they have in products such as cotton and sugar, because wealthier nations could no longer afford to flood the market and reduce prices. However, many countries will only benefit if they also reform and modernize their own systems to make it easier to trade. These systems include such

factors as customs procedures that can delay the import and export of goods and which can add significantly to the end cost of a product. Inefficiencies in the Indian port of Mumbai, for example, have been estimated to make Indian textile exports to the U.S. 37 percent more expensive than those from Shanghai in China. This is clearly a major disadvantage for Indian textile companies.

Have Your Say

Many argue that wealthier nations should make it their responsibility to ensure that LEDCs have better opportunities for global trade.

- Would greater trade for LEDCs benefit everyone?
- Should it really be the concern of wealthier countries to make trade easier for LEDCs?
- Will a single world trading system ever be good enough to meet the needs of all countries?

▼ In LEDCs such as Mexico, children rarely have the opportunity to complete elementary school, let alone learn the skills they would need to help support a global economy.

Making Trade Fair

No one is saying that trade is a bad idea—far from it. Trade can benefit everyone as long as they are given an equal chance to compete on the global market, and as long as workers are treated well and receive a fair price for their products. The pressure from campaigners to reform global trading systems focuses on making trade fair. Systems such as government subsidies are believed by many to go against the principles of fair trade. They protect industries in MEDCs and prevent those in poorer nations from selling goods in those markets. In a similar way, some companies that move to other countries to take advantage of cheap labor in factories

Focus on...
Cooperatives

The Woman's Multi-Purpose Cooperative is a fair-trade organization based near Manila in the Philippines. It was set up in 1997 to help women in the region earn a decent living and to help improve the local economy. The women who belong to the cooperative are provided with fair wages, safe working conditions, and reasonable working hours, as well as a food allocation. They are offered training and personal development seminars. There is also a scholarship fund to help local children receive a good education. Children are not allowed to work for the cooperative, which means they are not exploited. The cooperative makes items such as bags and lunchboxes out of recycled material, and these are exported to other countries.

▼ This woman is selling clothes at a fair-trade market in the UK. The clothes have been produced in decent working conditions by people who have received a fair wage.

Fairtrade Sales Volume (2004/2005)

Product sales	Sales volume 2004	Sales volume 2005	Growth in %
Tea	2,165 tons (1,964 t)	2,883 tons (2,615 t)	33
Coffee	26,700 tons (24,222 t)	37,469 tons (33,991 t)	40
Bananas	88,891 tons (80,641 t)	114,505 tons (103,877 t)	29
Fresh fruit	5,685 tons (5,157 t)	9,137 tons (8,289 t)	61
Sugar	2,162 tons (1,961 t)	3,983 tons (3,613 t)	84
Honey	1,370 tons (1,240 t)	1,470 tons (1,330 t)	7
Juices	5,008 tons (4,543 t)	6,501 tons (5,898 t)	30
Rice	1,524 tons (1,383 t)	1,878 tons (1,704 t)	23
Cocoa	4,630 tons (4,201 t)	6,236 tons (5,657 t)	35
Flowers*	101,610	113,536	12
Wine	163,191 gallons (617,744 l)	298,384 gallons (1,129,508 l)	83
Cotton	–	1,545 tons (1,402 t)	–
Dried fruit	262 tons (238 t)	337 tons (306 t)	29
Sport balls**	55,219	64,114	16

* Stems / ** Items

▲ This table shows the increase in sales of certain fair trade products in the space of just one year.

or call centers are criticized for paying such low wages that many see it almost a modern form of slavery.

The Fair-Trade Movement

It will be a long and difficult process to make all global trade fair, but there are ways that all consumers can make a difference. The fair-trade movement is a group of national consumer labeling organizations that promote goods traded on fair-trade principles. These principles involve working with local people in LEDCs to ensure a fair price for their goods and longer-term stability for their businesses. By guaranteeing the price farmers will receive for their coffee or cocoa, for example, the farmer is able to plan more confidently and avoid the uncertainty of the "unfair" open markets. The difference may only be a few cents per pound, but for local farmers this might mean they can be sure of sending their children to school, or perhaps give them enough income to invest in expanding their business. The fair-trade movement has grown enormously over the last 20 years, from a relatively minor organization involving just a few goods into an international network with thousands of products. Food products remain the most common fair-trade products, but in Europe, fair-trade flowers, clothing, and even sports equipment are available. In 2006, consumers spent about $2.2 billion worldwide on certified trade products, a 42% increase over 2005.

Eyewitness

"We rely on the money we get from cocoa for everything: for food, clothes, medicines, and school fees. Getting payment for our cocoa beans used to be very hit and miss. When we didn't get paid, we went without. Kuapa Kokoo pays all its farmers a fair price for their crop, in cash, and on time. I am very happy: since I joined Fair Trade I can afford to send my children to school."
Lucy Mansa, cocoa farmer in Kuapa Kokoo cooperative, Ghana

▲ The Fairtrade label shows buyers that the product has been produced in a way that benefits the individuals and communities that have originated it.

Behind the Label

Fairly traded products carry a label to show consumers that they meet the principles of fair trade and benefit local communities. If retailers want to use the label on their products, then they must buy from producers registered with their national labeling organization. By 2007, 20 countries had labeling initiatives registered with the Fairtrade Labelling Organizations International (FLO), the body that monitors such programs. They included the U.S., Canada, Australia, New Zealand, the UK, Spain, France, and Japan. By 2006, fair-trade initiatives registered with FLO were working directly with some five million people (farmers, workers, and their families) in 58 countries, and their retail value was increasing by around 40 percent a year.

Does It Make a Difference?

Many fair-trade campaigns focus on the real difference that purchasing fair-trade products can have on producers and their families. Individual families have certainly benefited from their involvement in fair-trade initiatives, but some question the overall effectiveness of the fair-trade movement and whether it can really make a difference. It has been successful in some markets, such as the coffee market in the United Kingdom. By 2006, Fairtrade coffee accounted for 18 percent of fresh coffee sales and 4 percent of sales of instant coffee. In the U.S., only 3.3

Eyewitness

"This is a turning point for us and for the coffee growers. This just shows what we, the public, can achieve. Here is a major multinational listening to people and giving them what they want—a Fairtrade product."

Harriet Lamb, director of the Fairtrade Foundation (UK), talking about the launch of Nescafé Fairtrade coffee in the UK

percent of coffee sold in 2006 was certified fairtrade. But that is more than eight times the amount sold in 2001. The vast majority of coffee sold in the U.S., UK, and throughout the world still comes from the 25 million or so independent growers throughout the world.

Supporters of fair trade argue that the pressure and influence of the idea is what can make the difference. In late 2005, for example, Nescafé, one of the world's largest coffee producers and a major TNC, announced it was launching a Fairtrade coffee. Other leading companies in coffee and other products have made similar moves, or in some cases have made their own fair-trade policies. Without ongoing pressure of the fair-trade movement, it is less likely these actions would have been taken.

While welcoming these changes, campaigners point out that real difference will come when

Have Your Say

If we all bought fair-trade products then we would make a real difference to global trade.

- Is buying a fair-trade product enough? How much does it really change?
- If most profit is made from processing goods, doesn't fair trade still benefit the retailers most? How could this be changed?
- How much more should we pay for fair-trade goods? Should unfair goods be taxed?

the focus turns to unfair trade. For example, cocoa farmers working in a cooperative may well benefit from better prices for the sale of raw cocoa to Europe, but they would have to pay a 25 percent tariff on that same cocoa if they processed it before selling it. Most of the profit from cocoa is made by processing it into higher-value chocolate products, and so this unfair tariff puts cocoa producers at a major disadvantage.

▼ These women in Nicaragua work on a fair-trade coffee plantation. They are checking the coffee beans and removing any bad ones, to make sure the coffee will be of a high quality.

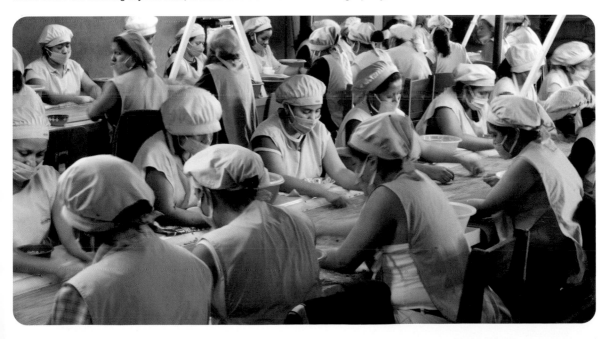

The Bigger Picture

Removing unfair tariffs or subsidies will require political decisions, in addition to social pressure from fair-trade or other campaign groups. Countries such as Brazil, India, China, and South Africa are currently taking a lead role in campaigning for fairer global trading conditions that benefit not just farmers, but global trade in general. The impact of such changes could be significant. It has been predicted, for example, that just a one percent growth in Africa's share of global trade would increase annual export earnings for the continent by $70 billion. This is several times greater than the current aid budgets going into Africa each year.

Eyewitness

"We reaffirmed our commitment to open markets more widely to trade in agricultural goods, industrial goods and services, and in agriculture, to reduce trade distorting domestic subsidies and eliminate all forms of export subsidies by a credible end date. We also committed to address products of interest to Least Developed Countries in the negotiations, and to ensure Least Developed Countries have the flexibility to decide their own economic strategies."
G8 summit statement, 2005

▼ Heads of state of the G8 countries meet in Germany in June 2007. The possibility of canceling the debts of some LEDCs was under discussion at the G8 meetings.

Major changes to the system such as these will require the cooperation of the WTO and the world's major trading blocs. The Group of Eight (G8) countries (U.S., Japan, UK, Germany, France, Russia, Italy, Canada, and representation from the European Union) is a particularly powerful group, whose decisions have a major impact on global trade.

In 2005, G8 leaders met in the UK to discuss whether agricultural subsidies should be removed and debt canceled for the poorest countries in the world. Campaigners celebrated this as a major achievement. By canceling the debts of some LEDCs, there would be more money for them to spend on health care, education, and infrastructure such as water, roads, and electricity. Such investments have been a vital factor in the success of other countries where trade and incomes have improved. They help to attract higher levels of foreign investment and create stronger local markets.

Creating Equality

Although canceling debt is not directly related to trade, it is an example of how policies can have broader effects. Many of the negative issues associated with the globalization of trade arise because poorer countries simply cannot compete on an equal footing with wealthier countries. Many experts argue that creating a more equal global society would increase the size of markets and open up new opportunities for trade. There is much evidence to suggest this is true, but only if it is accompanied by efforts to remove unfair trading structures and reform institutions like the World Trade Organization.

Focus on...
Going Local

An interesting reaction to the growing globalization of trade has been an increase in localization. This is where people and communities have become disillusioned with globalization and the lack of choice or closure of local businesses that this can mean. Instead, they try to buy goods that benefit local people. One sign of this trend is the increasing popularity of farmers markets, where local producers come together to sell their produce direct to the public. In the U.S., there were more than 4,000 regular farmers markets operating in 2007. Evidence suggests that as well as benefiting local farmers, customers visiting the markets increase local trade by up to 30 percent, benefiting a wide range of local retailers.

▼ In countries such as India, local markets have always been part of everyday life and trade. This trend is now becoming more popular in MEDCs.

The Great Debate

Global trade has become faster and cheaper as a result of globalization. For millions of people, this has meant greater choice and lower prices, but for others, it has meant the loss of jobs and the closure of businesses. Many of the rules controlling global trade remain controversial, and the current system is said to benefit only a wealthy few. At the beginning of the twenty-first century, we are all dependent on global trade for the lifestyles we have become used to. This brings many advantages, but there are just as many disadvantages.

Advantages include:

● Greater competition at a global level has lowered the costs of many goods and services.

● The ability to choose where and from whom you purchase goods and services. The Internet has made this truly global.

● The introduction of new products and services that were previously unavailable.

● Greater choice—supermarkets today stock a much wider range of goods than they did 10 years ago, for example.

● Year-round availability of goods that were previously considered seasonal.

● Opportunities for countries with few natural resources to develop their economies based on trade.

● The growth of a global fair-trade movement that ensures producers are treated and paid fairly.

● New opportunities for even small companies or individuals to trade at a global level.

Disadvantages include:

● Unfair systems of tariffs and subsidies that benefit the already wealthy and powerful countries and disadvantage LEDCs.

● Many of the largest companies involved in global trade have become more powerful than countries. How much power do they have over our lives?

● Local businesses have been forced to close because they are unable to compete with larger global companies.

● Millions of people are trapped in low-paying jobs because global trade puts huge pressure on keeping costs low. In some countries, wages are too low for people to afford basic needs.

● The environmental impact of global trade and in particular the movement of goods across vast distances.

● The tendency of profits to be relocated to the home nation of global companies, leaving few benefits for the host country.

Facts and Figures

The 20 Largest Global Companies by Market Value (2007)

Company	Country of origin	Type of business	Market value ($ billion)
ExxonMobil	United States	Oil and gas operations	410.65
General Electric	United States	Conglomerates	358.98
Microsoft	United States	Software and services	275.85
Citigroup	United States	Banking	247.42
AT&T	United States	Telecommunications services	229.78
Bank of America	United States	Banking	226.61
Toyota Motor	Japan	Consumer durables	217.69
Gazprom	Russia	Oil and gas operations	216.14
PetroChina	China	Oil and gas operations	208.70
Royal Dutch Shell	Netherlands	Oil and gas operations	208.25
HSBC Holdings	United Kingdom	Banking	202.29
Wal-Mart Stores	United States	Retailing	201.36
Procter & Gamble	United States	Household and personal products	200.34
BP	United Kingdom	Oil and gas operations	198.14
China Mobile	Hong Kong/China	Telecommunications services	185.31
Johnson & Johnson	United States	Drugs and biotechnology	182.12
Pfizer	United States	Drugs and biotechnology	179.97
Altria Group	United States	Food, drink and tobacco	176.64
ICBC	China	Banking	176.03
American Intl Group	United States	Insurance	174.47

Merchandise Exports as Percentage of World Total (2005)

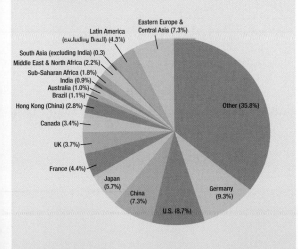

Eastern Europe & Central Asia (7.3%)
Latin America (excluding Brazil) (4.5%)
South Asia (excluding India) (0.3)
Middle East & North Africa (2.2%)
Sub-Saharan Africa (1.8%)
India (0.9%)
Australia (1.0%)
Brazil (1.1%)
Hong Kong (China) (2.8%)
Canada (3.4%)
UK (3.7%)
France (4.4%)
Japan (5.7%)
China (7.3%)
U.S. (8.7%)
Germany (9.3%)
Other (35.8%)

Source: World Bank

- Number of countries in the World Trade Organization: **150 (2007)**
- Value of global merchandise exports: **$10,434 billion (2005)**
- Value of global merchandise imports: **$10,685 billion (2005)**
- Number of national fair-trade labeling organizations: **21 (2007)**
- Growth in sales of fair-trade labeled products: **37 percent (2004–2005)**

Further Information

Books

Cooper, Adrian. *Fair Trade?* Issues of the World. North Mankato, Minn.: Stargazer Books, 2006.

Downing, David. *Global Business: Who Benefits?* Behind the News. Chicago: Heinemann Library, 2007.

Harris, Nathaniel. *The Debate About Globalization.* Ethical Debates. New York: Rosen Central, 2008.

Hibbert, Adam. *Globalization.* Chicago: Raintree, 2005.

January, Brendan. *Globalize It!: The Stories of the IMF, the World Bank, the WTO, and Those Who Protest.* Brookfield, Conn.: Twenty-First Century Books, 2003.

Web Sites

www.webforum.org/en/index.htm
The website of the World Economic Forum, with all the latest news on how the problems associated with globalization are being addressed.

www.citizen.org/trade/
The site for Global Trade Watch (GTW), an organization promoting democracy by challenging corporate globalization.

www.transfairusa.org/
TransFair USA, a nonprofit organization, is one of twenty members of Fairtrade Labeling Organizations International (FLO), and the only third-party certifier of fair trade products in the U.S.

www.wto.org/english/forums_e/students_e/students_e.htm
The student pages of the WTO provide good links to guide users in finding basic or detailed information about trade issues and the WTO.

www.fairtrade.net
The international labeling organization for the various national fair trade projects. Their site has information about the history and growth of fair trade products and sales.

www.organicconsumers.org/
The Organic Consumers Association (OCA) is an online and grassroots non-profit organization campaigning for health, justice, and sustainability. The OCA deals with issues of food safety, industrial agriculture, genetic engineering, children's health, corporate accountability, Fair Trade, environmental sustainability, and other key topics. It promotes the views and interests of the nation's estimated 50 million organic and socially responsible consumers.

Teaching Resources

www.loc.gov/rr/business/BERA/issue/history.html
A guide to Internet and print resources dedicated to the history of the world economy, including international trade, the foreign exchange market, and trade law.

www.oxfamamerica.org/whatyoucando/teachers
Oxfam's resources give teachers ideas on how to teach kids about the issues of globalization, poverty, and social and economic issues.

www.oxfam.org.uk/education/resources/milking_it/milkingit/
A website for teachers, with classroom activities that compare the lives of dairy farmers in Wales and Jamaica, demonstrating how they are both affected by trade issues.

www.ssrc.org/sept11/essays/teaching_resource/tr_globalization.htm
The Social Science Research Council provides essays, lesson plans, and teaching guides on topics such as globalization and terrorism.

Glossary

acquisition the process of buying or acquiring something. The word is normally used to describe the purchase of one company by another.

biotechnology technology that is based around or utilizes living organisms. Often related to developments in the fields of medicine and food.

colony a country or region that is ruled by a foreign government.

commodity an item that is bought or sold, normally in a raw or unprocessed state, such as tea, sugar, coffee, or minerals.

economy the supply of money gained by a community or country from goods and services.

entrepreneur an individual who sets up his or her own business.

export any good or service that is sold outside the country in which it originates.

fair trade trade that ensures producers are paid a fair and guaranteed price for their products, often with an additional premium to help fund social development such as education or health care.

foreign-exchange earnings money that a country earns by selling things.

free trade trade that takes place without the presence of tariffs or subsidies and which is based on the price that people are willing to pay.

General Agreement on Tariffs and Trade (GATT) an organization established in 1947 to reduce trade barriers and make trading between countries easier. It was succeeded in 1995 by the World Trade Organization.

genetically modified (GM) food a food item that contains matter that has had its natural genes modified by humans to improve some quality such as color, size, or resistance to drought or pests.

globalization the freedom of businesses to operate all over the world and to invest and employ workers wherever they choose.

import any good or service that originates from outside the country by which it is purchased.

less economically developed country (LEDC) one of the poorer countries of the world. LEDCs include all of Africa, Asia (except for Japan), Latin America and the Caribbean, and Melanesia, Micronesia, and Polynesia.

merger the process of two companies joining forces.

migration the movement of people from one place to another (often from country to country) in order to live or find work. Migration can be temporary, seasonal, or permanent.

more economically developed country (MEDC) one of the richer countries of the world. MEDCs include all of Europe, northern America, Australia, New Zealand, and Japan.

quota a limit on the amount of a product that can be imported into a country. Quotas are often used to protect domestic producers from cheaper or competing imported goods.

recession a period of economic decline or very slow growth.

remittances money sent by a relative working abroad to his or her family back home.

resource something of value that can be put to a particular use—oil, coal, and copper are examples of natural resources.

sanctions actions taken against a specific country (normally involving trade) in order to force them into complying with an international agreement. The WTO can impose trade sanctions, for example.

subsidy a financial benefit paid to a producer as an incentive to produce. Subsidies are normally paid by government bodies and are especially used in farming.

tariff a monetary payment (tax) charged by a government on imported (and sometimes exported) goods.

tax a monetary payment charged by a government to businesses and/or individuals and used to fund government activities and expenditures.

transnational corporation (TNC) a company that operates in more than one country. The term multinational corporation (MNC) is sometimes used as an alternative.

World Trade Organization (WTO) an organization that administers trade agreements, provides a forum for trade negotiations, and monitors national trade policies for the 150 member countries. The overall aim of the WTO is to reach a single set of rules for trade.

Index